Maths A...

Me...in
th...en

www.raintreepublishers.co.uk
Visit our website to find out
more information about
Raintree books.

To order:

☎ Phone 0845 6044371

🖹 Fax +44 (0) 1865 312263

🖳 Email myorders@raintreepublishers.co.uk

Customers from outside the UK please telephone +44 1865 312262

Raintree is an imprint of Capstone Global Library Limited,
a company incorporated in England and Wales having its
registered office at 7 Pilgrim Street, London, EC4V 6LB
– Registered company number: 6695582

Edited by Rebecca Rissman, Tracey Steffora, and Catherine Veitch
Designed by Joanna Hinton-Malivoire
Picture research by Elizabeth Alexander
Production by Victoria Fitzgerald
Originated by Capstone Global Library Ltd
Printed and bound in China by Leo Paper Products Ltd

ISBN 978 1 406 22319 4 (hardback)
15 14 13 12 11
10 9 8 7 6 5 4 3 2 1

ISBN 978 1 406 22327 9 (paperback)
16 15 14 13 12
10 9 8 7 6 5 4 3 2 1

British Library Cataloguing in Publication Data
Steffora, Tracey.
Measuring in the garden. -- (Maths around us)
530.8-dc22

Acknowledgements
The author and publisher are grateful to the following for
permission to reproduce photographs: © Capstone Publishers
p. 22 (Karon Dubke); Alamy pp. 7 (© Victor Watts), 19 (© Robert
Harrison); Corbis p. 5 (© Yi Lu); iStockphoto pp. 6 (© Elena
Elisseeva), 14 (© Carmen Martínez Banús); Photolibrary pp. 13 (Jochen
Tack/imagebroker.net), 18 (Garden Picture Library),
20 (Photos Lamontagne/Garden Picture Library), 21 (Michael
Freeman/Red Cover); Shutterstock pp. 4 (© Sternstunden), 6 inset (©
Christophe Testi), 8 (© Vitaly Romanovich), 9 (© Monkey
Business Images), 11 (© Kenneth Sponsler), 10 (© Gina Smith),
12 (© a40757), 15 (© Joe Gough), 16 (© Kokhanchikov), 17 (© master
stock), 23 glossary – earthworm (© Kokhanchikov), 23 glossary – soil
(© Monkey Business Images), 23 glossary –
temperature (© Christophe Testi).

Cover photograph of a girl watering a plant reproduced with
permission of Shutterstock (© Monkey Business Images). Back cover
photograph of a vegetable garden reproduced with
permission of iStockphoto (© Carmen Martínez Banús).

We would like to thank Nancy Harris, Dee Reid, and Diana Bentley for
their assistance in the preparation of this book.

Every effort has been made to contact copyright holders of
material reproduced in this book. Any omissions will be rectified in
subsequent printings if notice is given to the publisher.

Contents

Gardens

Many things grow in gardens.

We can help gardens grow.

How warm?

thermometer

We measure temperature to know when to plant.

Plants grow in warm weather.

We plant in spring and summer.

How much?

Plants grow in soil.

Large pots hold more soil.

soil

Small pots hold less soil.

water lily

Plants need water.

Some plants need more water.

cactus

Some plants need less water.

Plants need space.

Some plants need more space.

Some plants need less space.

How tall?

beans

lettuce

Plants can be different sizes.

The beans are taller than the lettuce.

The red flowers are taller than the white flowers.

How long?

Earthworms live in soil.

Earthworms are good for soil.

Which worm is longer?

Which worm is shorter?

How heavy?

Some gardens have rocks.

Rocks can be small and light.

Rocks can be big and heavy.

Gardens everywhere

This garden is on a wall.

This garden is on a roof.

Planting seeds

Plants need space to grow. Use your hand to measure a space between

each seed or plant.

Picture glossary

 **earthworm** worm that lives in damp earth or soil

 **soil** loose part of the earth in which plants grow

 **temperature** measure of how warm or cold something is

Index

Notes for parents and teachers

Before reading

Young children first begin to understand measurement through comparisons. Provide children with opportunities to experience and use vocabulary such as more and less, longer and shorter, heavier and lighter, or bigger and smaller. Discuss how we measure and compare things in our environment all the time, even if we are not using formal measuring tools such as rulers or scales.

After reading

• Plant seeds with children, utilizing vocabulary of size, weight, height, and volume.

• Take a walk in your neighbourhood or community and look for gardens. These might be found in a park or in a window box. Discuss how plants can grow in many places and discuss the important role they play in our world (supplying food, oxygen, beauty, etc.)